ROOMS BY DESIGN

GERD HATJE AND HERBERT WEISSKAMP

ROOMS BY DESIGN

HARRY N. ABRAMS, INC., PUBLISHERS, NEW YORK

Editor: Alexandra Bonfante-Warren
Designer: Maria Miller

Library of Congress Cataloging-in-Publication Data
Hatje, Gerd.
   Rooms by Design / Gerd Hatje and Herbert Weisskamp.
      p.   cm.
   ISBN 0–8109–1598–7
      1. Interior decoration–20th century.   I. Weisskamp,
Herbert. II. Title.
NK 1980.H37   1989
728′.09′04—dc 19   88–34857

The Elliott house *(see page 2)* in Ligonier, Pennsylvania, seems literally to embrace the visitor—a Renaissance architectural effect. Jefferson B. Riley of Moore, Grove, Harper here combined other traditional elements as well: the Classical Greek atrium, the Victorian conservatory, and the timeless entrance hall.

Riley tastefully implemented Post-Modernism in the library *(see page 5)*. The hand-carved overmantel rises like curling smoke into the paneled upper reaches of the room. Fantasy suggests a tepee. Practicality dictated the ladder on a fine brass track. Tradition prompted the choice of a green-shaded lamp.

The warm tint and low luster of the wooden flooring is repeated in the vertical rails of the gallery above *(see page 6)*, but only at intervals in the ceiling treatment. The elaborate manner of the chinoiserie contrasts with the naturalist leaves and whorls of the walls.

Riley's design for the kitchen *(see page 8)* nestles a room within a room, negotiating between the two to the advantage of the whole. For example, the turret is fairy-tale charming; it is also the tallest wooden element in the space, and bridges the two sets of proportions. The stacked windows flood the room with light by day. By night, lamps not only provide illumination where needed, but create a second, lower ceiling.

INTRODUCTION

It seems to be innate to our species to arrange, discover, and otherwise create pleasing and ever-changing environments. Outdoors, our parks, skyscrapers, gardens, and malls are devised to invite our admiration and patronage. Indoors, in offices, restaurants, stores, and other public spaces, we use design to encourage and enhance the activities these places are intended to host. ▨ In our homes we pursue an ongoing process of transformation. It happens when we devise different table settings or have fresh flowers every day, when we change upholstery and draperies with the seasons. But sometimes it happens when we become suddenly aware that we have evolved and that our rooms must, too, if they are to continue to express us and restore us. ▨ Interior design is a discipline—sometimes an art—that is just beginning to come into its own as a popular resource, not just a luxury for a select group of professional architects, designers, and decorators. ▨ As recently as twenty-five years ago, interior design was synonymous with a rigid set of requirements by which we judged and were judged. We were ruled by a narrow range of color schemes, of contours, of seating arrangements, and woe be to the nonconformist! ▨ Today, when it sometimes seems that anything goes, we may be overwhelmed by the very multitude of our options. We want to be of our time—but not slaves to style; classical—but not *déjà vu*. Where do we begin? ▨ We begin by realizing that redoing our rooms is an important process that merits our time and attention. Furthermore, it is a process that we must enjoy, for the enthusiasm and pleasure we feel for the task will surely be reflected in the results, adding a dimension that money can't buy. ▨ What is the scope of our project? If we are rearranging the flow of space, we may decide to have (or keep) a cozy, boxy layout. We may want a single, vast space. One architect's solution was to cut a supporting wall back to a line of columns, thus allowing both a flow of light and separate rooms. ▨ Many of us agree with the ancient Greek belief that correct proportions are divinely inspired. If we can't actually build our homes from scratch, we can use furniture groupings, room dividers, dropped ceilings, platforms, or a number of devices to create satisfying proportions. ▨ If we set our imaginations to it, we can even have gardens in our homes. One tiny Milan studio boasts a luxuriant corner garden, while a more formal apartment breaks through the exterior wall to incorporate the balcony into a glassed-in alcove. The new space accommodates a window seat and a profusion of hanging plants, for a manageable contemporary conservatory. ◪ The reason why modernism has endured so long—particularly in residential design—is that it is humanely flexible. Easy maintenance is one of its principal reasons for being, conceived as it was for the newly servantless middle class following World War I. That same reductiveness translates today into a neutral background for a graceful and personal eclecticism. ◪ Our process demands that we look everywhere, in order to explore a variety of styles and our own tastes. We look to the timeless serenity of traditional Japanese interiors, to the French Empire, and to homes in the Italian countryside and the German forests. We study the many design books and magazines available. We return to our favorite museums and investigate new ones. ◪ If it seems a leap from the decorative arts to the fine arts, we should recall that the line between them occasionally has been a blurred one. The Etruscan frescoes we travel thousands of miles to admire were, in long-ago homes, the adornment of rooms in which people entertained family and friends, sewed, listened to music, dined, and lived. Tapestries once warmed chilly stone walls. For some, Ottavio Missoni's wall hangings are the modern-day equivalent. ◪ In the last century, William Morris married art and craft in interior design. And what is Art Deco but a streamlined abbreviation of *art décoratif*? Today, the serviceable kitchen appliance we use every day may have pride of place in a museum of modern art. ◪ Here, in the very availability of high-quality decorative art and industrial design, lies one of the pitfalls that await the unwary. At one extreme is the overdecorated house. We may be seduced by a charming look (that turns out to be a trend-of-the-month) or by a too-coordinated assembly that makes us feel like Goldilocks intruding upon someone else's taste. ◪ Less easily avoided, perhaps, is the other extreme: the room that contains all and only our favorite things. Instead of a warmly cheerful mix, we—bafflingly—find ourselves in an undifferentiated jumble where pieces lose the very uniqueness that endears them to us. ◪ For each room, let us choose a focus around which the room's spatial relations will be organized. A fireplace, for instance, can act as the major piece, with secondary focuses—two pictures—on either side. ◪ If we have the space, we may lavishly devote a room to a few special pieces. In an entrance hall, Rietveld's classic Red and Blue Chair is placed in relation to a Dutch Baroque cupboard—to the advantage of both. Here, it is not focus, but juxtaposition that operates successfully. ◪ A color or palette of colors can unify a room. An orange carpet brings together a series of rooms with ivory walls and red and matte black accents. ▤ When we know clearly what the purpose is (or purposes are, in an age when space is the ultimate luxury) of a room, then we are well on our way. If we want a separate dining room, then we may want to formalize it with, for example, a deep-chocolate-brown wall treatment highlighted with bright white moldings. ▤ Formality in a sweeping rectangular room that contains dining room and living room in sequence becomes something quite eloquent. The contrast between open plan and traditional setting becomes striking indeed. ▤ Looking to myriad and often unexpected sources of ideas around us shakes some of our preconceptions. The freer we are of preconceived notions, the more at home we will be at home. ▤ Curiously, it is one of the newer rooms in the history of homes that is also the one most taken for granted: the bathroom. We may find pleasure in a bathroom that takes traditional notions of hygiene to extremes in a neon-lit glare of white tile. Perhaps we find sensual delight in a long soak in a deep, old-fashioned claw-foot tub. As long as we are spending time there, why not mark the room off with a drape of filet and an artwork that says that this is a room to spend time in? In a single long room, a designer separates the bathroom from the living room only by a ceiling-high door on one side, and a low counter. Most of us, though, will prefer the middle ground—but even the middle ground is a treasure trove of charming notions! ▤ The more we explore our inner requirements, as well as our external ones, the more we will be nurtured by our rooms. And if those rooms are as wildly colorful as artist Keith Haring's, awash with graffiti and psychedelia and a flying horse, then all the better. ▤ Play is as essential to us as it is to our children. An aristocratic home turned out to be quirkily and elegantly adaptable to two collectors' most beloved pieces, ranging from those of the most modern of the pre–World War II designers to classic Memphis creations. ▤ And if we live with children, then what could be more right than to construct rooms that welcome all who play there—adults *and* children? A spare television alcove off of a landing can easily reconcile a Warhol silkscreen of Marilyn Monroe and a Mickey Mouse rocking horse, especially when—by choice or chance?—they are in the same colors. ▤ If there is a single key word in design today, that word must be *choice*. This book was written in the belief that this is the best of times to reevaluate our homes' interiors, when we may draw unselfconsciously from the best of *all* times and places to create rooms that are uniquely, personally ours. ▤

In the eighties, subtle new considerations began entering our rooms: textures, sounds—even scents—are enriching our environments. No longer are our homes "statements"—assertive and hard-edged—yet still they say a great deal, and with wit, comfort, and style. ▨ For most of us, it is prohibitively time-consuming and expensive to assemble perfect settings of period pieces. We may prefer to find a single antique we love and integrate it into an overall scheme that enhances it. In

PERIODS IN CONTRAST

that way our rooms become interplays of epochs, as well as of space, when we add, delete, and collect, following the lead of the Empress Eugénie, who began the practice of selecting from the wealth of the past and present. ▨ If we look around our rooms, we will rediscover architectural elements that we previously took for granted. Hand-hewn wood beams, pressed-tin ceilings, and ornate moldings take on fresh new interest when they frame sleek modern sofas, industrial shelving—even relaxed arrangements of informal pieces. Conversely, stark contemporary walls can embrace the elaborate fragility of an eighteenth-century chandelier or the massive gravity of a dark oak *cassone* to its most elegant advantage. ▨ Color can evoke rich connotations of the past. A sultry Pompeian-red accent, for example, breathes luxury, urbanity, and civilized sensuality. It endows a dining room with a welcoming warmth—and its guests, if the traditional belief be true, with healthy appetites. Earth hues can be surprisingly inviting, as can a range of whites, ivories, or creams, in matte finishes or glowing enamels. ▨ Materials can delight with unexpected uses. Draped filet in a bathroom emphasizes the old-fashioned solemnity of a deep porcelain tub. Beams and moldings, arches and columns, and fabrics can sculpt our surroundings. An openwork lacquer grid answers itself harmonically in the mirror above the classical curves of a marble fireplace; a floral-print extravagance in a bedroom provides a strikingly effective contrast with a few carefully placed antiques. ▨ When, with an open and loving eye, we add the dimension of time to tint, texture, and shape, the whole is far greater than the sum of its parts. Even a single flourish—a sweep of fabric suggesting a regal canopy, a modest but cherished family heirloom— brings history into our homes, adding character to the way we live. ▨

(see picture on preceding spread)

At the patriarchal center of Old Milan, architects Mario Tedeschi and Gianpaolo Monti designed an entrance hall that frames the angularity of Gerrit Rietveld's Red and Blue Chair and the imposing curved volume of an inlaid Dutch Baroque cupboard.

The dining room *(above)*, which Tedeschi and Monti designed after the owners returned to Milan from the Orient, features a concrete-and-glass dining table adorned with Chinese plates and surrounded by Giorgetti's Chinese-red lacquer chairs. The fairy-tale chandelier is eighteenth-century Murano glass. The red-framed wall hanging—a spectrum of tones and textures by Ottavio Missoni—dominates the spare elegance of the room.

W hims of boudoir in the bath. A remark-
able filet curtain transforms this bathroom from old-fashioned to *fin-de-siècle;*
a vertically striped wall treatment enhances
the effect. The sensuous folds of a relief in
epoxy strikes a graceful Post-Modern note.
This is an alcove for reading, for soaking, for
dreaming one's cares away.

Berlin architect Axel Schultes was not permitted to make structural alterations to his turn-of-the-century home. Instead, he devised movable "towers"—industrial shelving on casters. Holding record albums, lamps, stereo components, or a typewriter, these rooms on wheels can define the function of an area, a contemporary design notion that Schultes has integrated into the ornate gentility of another age.

Schultes reworks time-honored floor plans, allowing a reception area, for example, to flow into a bedroom. Continuity is suggested by the parquet and by the use of a single style for the chair and couches.

French doors to the upstairs gallery of the Elliott house are a play of outside–in— the gallery continues beyond the exterior walls *(see first four pictures at the front of book)*. The living room is turned on an axis: a traditional room layout would place the wing chairs on either side of the fireplace. Here, Jefferson B. Riley has used the chairs, two delicate occasional tables, and the border of the carpet to mark the outer edge of the area.

An architect built this high-domed, chapel-like studio for himself in 1931. Today, designed by Didier Aaron and Jacques Grange, this space accommodates simultaneously the traditional and the avant-garde, the art of the Orient and of Europe. Far from diluting the effect of each piece, the knowledgeable juxtaposition of pictures enhances each one.

Brass and green marble combine in sumptuous geometry at one end of a New York City living and dining room by architect and designer Leslie Armstrong. She plotted a play of depths and color that supports the works of art in the room.

(apartment continues overleaf)

(continued from preceding spread)

Armstrong subtly unites the two areas with the warm-on-cool ambience of candlelight on satin. She has selected period touches to enhance the opulence: handsomely wrought candlesticks, a brass-and-alabaster lamp base. The sparkling silver draperies are backdrops from a photographer's studio.

Designer Francis Prat's allusive decor ranges worldwide for its cosmopolitan effect. The black lacquer screen's Oriental origins relate it to the ceramics on the table in front of it. Beyond it on the far wall a thoroughly Western fireplace interrupts with its graceful curves the line of pictures to which the screen's grid calls attention.

Claudio Dini's design for an eighteenth-century villa in Lombardy places a window, within the suggestion of an arch, near the floor. An exposed beam, rich with character, defines the bookshelf wall. Soft lighting and flowers ease the pristine beauty of the white-on-white design.

(apartment continues overleaf)

(continued from preceding spread)

Dini's use of white tile everywhere is an urbane solution that implies the ease of country weekends. Against such a background, the paintings might seem quirky; instead, they have the pride of place they deserve.

Carl Hermann Wibbe, architect, has successfully balanced the dining and living areas in this house near the Ruhr. The delicate blue and white set off the artworks, all placed at eye-level, their lower borders aligned. In the living area, the furniture is comfortably modern, while Biedermeier pieces adorn the dining room table.

Karl Lagerfeld asked designer Andrée Putman to go beyond interior decoration in her treatment of his Paris apartment near the Louvre. Lagerfeld wanted "eighteen tones of gray, like the sky over the Seine" and furniture custom-made for his thousand books and magazines. Putman christened her creation "the brutal look." All the furniture is made of tubing. The bookcases and tables are on casters and can be moved as whim or necessity demands. On the mantel, in lieu of knick-knacks, is an array of electronic equipment.

(overleaf)

The New York firm of Smith & Thompson dovetailed the requirements of a modern-day workplace with a fanciful suggestion of a nineteenth-century shipping office. By building the drafting table into an alcove and angling the massive oak desk, the architects gave the latter center stage. The picture in the alcove is enough to suggest an era long gone by.

In an older town house on New York City's Gramercy Park West, architect John Fondrisi performed a design of apparent simplicity—and breathtaking effect. The black-and-white color scheme emphasizes the richly polished parquet and the ever-changing tracery of the park outside. There is a contrast of dimensions between the reliefs of the balcony ironwork and of the ceiling moldings and the cubic solidity of the Le Corbusier chairs.

Understated play: curves and linearity trade places *(top left)*. Severe shelves set off a plethora of bric-a-brac, while the splendor of a blank wall backs a mirrored, late Baroque headboard and the luster of fine embroidered silk. To the right of the bed, in a tiny alcove, two Baroque mirrors asymmetrically complement the stately bedstead.

Architect Piero Pinto's apartment *(bottom left)* in Milan breaks the rules—gently. A profusion of small flowers unifies the bedspread, draperies, and wall covering. The dim light lends a musing quality to a handful of books on an antique desk.

"Less is more," said Mies van der Rohe. "Less is a bore," countered Robert Venturi, godfather of Post-Modernism. In the reading room of his Philadelphia home *(above)*, every one of his favorite objects—discoveries made over the years across two continents—has its own story. The overmantel is a charming example of American Arts and Crafts; the grandfather clock comes from the French countryside.

The Eternal City itself is the focus of this narrow sitting room in the apartment of an art collector. Five hundred years of the pursuit of beauty are represented here: on the windowsill, a brass ball by Arnaldo Pomodoro echoes the curve of the arch above it; in the foreground, a Le Corbusier chaise longue allows one to contemplate the view; on the floor, handmade tiles bring Rome's unique, warm ocher inside.

(apartment continues overleaf)

Dark browns—the seventeenth-century sacristy cabinet, a deep sofa, and the oak piece in the foreground—line three walls. The room, a masterpiece of equilibrium, balances the antique brown woods with modern accents: two ivory couches and a pair of steel tube chairs by Marcel Breuer. The art ranges from a Baroque Potiphar to a red Fontana. In front of the window is a fanciful, blond-wood "chair sculpture" by Matta.

Whether it's in something as transitory as a flower arrangement, or as ambitious as a room designed to be art itself, our taste is always at work in the world. And however grand or modest our circumstances, we explore for the inspirations that stretch our imaginations and tap into our dreams. With what we find, we put together environments that nourish and refresh us. ▣ Everywhere around us are resources. Movies, magazines, and books are treasure troves of ideas. Museums of design and decorative arts focus on environments, while traditional museums offer us paintings depicting centuries of interiors. ▣ No longer are we compelled to choose between the beautiful and the utilitarian, between art and craft. Those are merely two points in the creative multiplicity of human activities—not opposites. When we follow our taste, our homes

ARTFUL
SCHEMES

show our feeling for beauty more successfully than if we were to follow this or that theory of interior design exclusively. ▣ A strict harmony of horizontals and verticals in a bare-bones loft will provide some people with the ease and sensual pleasure they seek in a room. For others, a room's main purpose will be to act as a backdrop for art and sculpture. ▣ Many of us, though—maybe most of us—prefer styles that look good, wear well, and are well made. (This is not a very strange notion in an age when chairs, typewriters, and ice buckets go into showrooms and museums simultaneously.) ▣ Most of us want to make environments for the art that we use and the art that we look at, listen to, and otherwise live with. Architecture has given us, for example, the mantel and the pedestal; both are time-honored places for favorite objects. Why shouldn't a set of classical architectural drawings surmount a classical fireplace, stimulating a well-bred double-take? Why shouldn't dark-brown pedestals sport stark-white sphinxes? ▣ Low tables are informal, contemporary places to display sculptures and beloved artifacts in charming, utterly personal arrays of pieces. (The contemporary designer David Hicks so prizes these "landscapes of objects" that he assigns their arrangement to master *assemblagistes*.) ▣ But color is, in the end, the magic ingredient. We may choose schemes of the glossiest white, the most velvety brown, the palest pastels—or an apparently random scattering of colors throughout the room. These colors may turn up in rugs, in upholstery, or on walls, but they will always, frankly or indirectly, frame and enhance the art in our lives. ▣

(see picture on preceding spread)

Finished in white cork, the dining room table in the Hamburg home of Swedish designer Eric Jacobson bears antique silver underplates, Plexiglas candlesticks, mother-of-pearl–lined shells, and white porcelain that combine to create a magical setting. Beyond, sweeps of Fortuny fabric drape to frame a marble obelisk.

The guest room *(above)* is a delight of honey tones. The ceiling-high closets, the Ceroli chair, the suede bedspread, and the carpet are dark and light elements. Like the other paintings throughout Jacobson's home, the blackberry-colored monochrome hangs at eye-level.

Jacobson does not care for the Nordic severity
so unsuited to the low, pearl-gray skies of this
Hanseatic city. The atmosphere beneath the
ornate stucco ceiling is warm, with little of
the ostentation of its original period. The parlor opens hospitably into both the dining room
and the more formal living room. Light sources
are at seat- or table-level.

In remodeling an older structure, architect Rodolfo Garattoni sought to give these rooms continuity despite their outsize proportions. Bookshelves and carpet achieved his purpose, as well as his use of two layers of color. The base color scheme uses earth tones—tobacco brown, pale green—for a sense of peace. These neutral tones, however, also enhance the colors in the artworks—including the multihued inlaid leather table. Pillows, books, and a tiny-patterned jacquard weave fabric on a couch all point to the framed "patterns" on the walls.

Ricardo Bofill's Paris apartment proves that less can be sumptuously more. The deep-red floor supports the pristine classicism of the fireplace—and of the architectural drawings above it.

Strong and imposing, the powerful presence of the black table is mitigated by the latticed grace of tall chairs. Poised above is the timeless elegance of a lamp, a curve rediscovered on the far wall. In blond frames, the two works of art are Bofill's plans for this home.

Leslie Armstrong has effected a relaxed and stylish atmosphere. She has installed three types of lighting, thereby giving the residents of this apartment on New York's Upper West Side a highly flexible system. The subtle gray green of the wall perfectly frames the painting. There is, too, classic American understatement in the symmetry of sconces and outlined door frames. The recessed lamps bring out the luster of fine antique English silver.

The contrasting taupe-and-ivory color scheme emphasizes the elaborate ceiling molding, just as the lighting accentuates the art in two and three dimensions. Yves Taralon, working in a nineteenth-century apartment in Paris's Plaine Monçeau, has unified the diversity with the rhythm of the vertical chairbacks, their blond wood allying them to the stark carpentry of the dining table.

Fluted columns of light double as pedestals in Klaus Reymann's playful and sophisticated wall treatment. The objects displayed appear to float—as do the glasses and bottles in the backlit bar recess. The Josef Hoffmann fabric on the wall forms a harmonious surround for the classic Viennese lines of the table and chairs.

nspired by his homeland, Italian-born designer Danilo Silvestrin devised for his Munich client a star-crowned *bel gioco di tetti*—a fine play of roofs. The diffuse white glow from the windows merges with the warmer light from the baseboard horizon.

The see-through chimneypiece overlooks a Munich skyline. The sides are a glissando of pastels that sum up the surrounding decor. Within, a campfire blazes its ancient spell behind an ultramodern glass hearth.

Sloping oval windows take the living room into the far reaches of a cheerful futurism. The range hood and other details—such as the cupboard handles—are treated with extreme reserve, in keeping with the elegantly muted color scheme.

What might have been kitsch is instead a pleasing and original environment. The starry firmament and soft pastels are anchored by the matte finish and angular geometry of the surfaces and by the soberly handsome dove gray of the floor tiles.

(apartment continues overleaf)

At the turn of the twenty-first century, the ultimate urban luxury is space. Here, levels, diagonals, and skylights cut into the ceiling: the whole is a triumph of cosmopolitan musicality.

Mimi Klein lives and works in her Munich apartment, designed by herself and Stefan Wewerka. As witty as it is practical, a tiled panel, reading like a minimalist mosaic, defines the understated galley kitchen. The counter on the right doubles as a bar. Black and white and red (here, the couch in the background) are the color themes that recur throughout the space.

Nestled together, a coffee table and couch recall the kidney shapes of the fifties. On the left, a metal stem supports a functional and flexible light source. Humorously, the video camera is mounted as if to videotape the television watchers.

(apartment continues overleaf)

53

(continued from preceding spread)

Art and the unexpected are everywhere, from the plywood floor to a chair like a farm implement blown in a gale. Indeed, the vertical beechwood paneling provides a deceptively conventional background for the art dealer Klein's wares, like the legless red table that seems to float behind a cylindrical lamp.

(apartment continues overleaf)

(continued from preceding spread)

Stripes and the intricate tracery of Tiffany set the tone for the contrasts at work in the conversation area. On an inset square of blue Brazilian stone stands the largest table lamp Louis Tiffany ever created. Stefan Wewerka's geometric chairs invite relaxed conversation, while corresponding red stripes on a platform against the wall conceal storage bins. The stripes continue to the frame of a case displaying Art Nouveau glassware.

A sudden, floral harmony of pastels appears on the wall and is repeated in the decoration of a column. A partial chair clasps the column just above the base.

eter Walser, architect and designer, created a home in which art dominates the
scene. Characteristic of much of the wall-
hung art in Walser's rooms is a suggestion of
the third dimension. The white of one wall
supports the texture of a white-on-white
painting, on the other wall, a feathery swirl
of dusty rose.

New reception rooms keep appearing—
private spaces, each with its own spirit, yet
unambiguously part of the whole. The prolif-
eration of modern furniture is rich and
diverse; the antiques infuse them with continuity and restraint. The armchairs are Louis
XV and Louis XVI, the white leather divan
is by Mies van der Rohe. White candles enhance the collection of silver candlesticks.

(apartment continues overleaf)

What seems so effortlessly attuned is the result
of thought and artistry. Closets vanished into
walls. The white-on-white scheme was a
triumph of persistence: marble is a product of
nature, whose infinite variety does not
always conform to the needs of designers.

Designer Barbara Schwartz, ASID, created a photo gallery in a beige-accented,
burgundy bedroom. The works of art are lit
museum-style by lamps on tracks. The bed, a
contemporary interpretation of the Murphy
bed, folds up during the day.

ves Taralon's kaleidoscopic reflections give us the bathroom as art. The Parisian designer established a dense blue that easily sustains the rhythmic bands of red. Glints of white and chrome relieve the eye.

Luca de Padova's Milan apartment was designed in collaboration with fellow architects Francesco Ridolfi and Patrizia Cagliani. Ease, technology, art, and fun come together in the living room. The industrial-style shelves are colorfully balanced by a papier-mâché rocking horse, a Moroccan rug, and a mixed-media composition of rice paper, photographs, and tempera. The furniture is fifties and sixties Dansk.

Reflected in Man Ray's oval mirror is a view of the dining room. There appears, as if in close-up, the grid motif of the lighting support, which also acts as a dropped ceiling. The scrawled inscription reads "*les grands trans-Parents*"—"the great trans-Parents."

(apartment continues overleaf)

The dining room embodies a good-humored marriage of cool functionalism and eighties Dada. Two female images are paired—a store mannequin and a Roy Lichtenstein comic-book heroine. Squares and primary colors are used throughout.

Entering the hall of the Hudin home in Paris, one discovers a stylish mix of reality and illusion. Expensive materials, modern art, and traditional architecture merge seamlessly in a singular unity—a project by architect Gaetano Pesce.

(apartment continues on next four pages)

Where does art end and the everyday begin? A row of bulbs is set below a sleeping alcove *(overleaf).* Flanked by paintings, the alcove itself becomes a tableau. The sedate moldings crowning the Post-Modern rambunctiousness add an ironic touch.

The sleeping room looks like a surrealistic stage set *(second overleaf, left):* the brown "package" and far-from-naturalistic stone wall behind it are visually arresting. Do they mean something? Only the inhabitants can say.

Asymmetry is the unifying aesthetic of the apartment *(second overleaf, top right).* The doors on this wall are out of kilter, in a tribute to imaginative anarchy. The sketched figure—observed by the red face in profile above her—is complete only when the door is closed.

Dramatic lacquered planes of black, red, and white startle with their abstraction *(second overleaf, bottom right),* after the riot of images elsewhere in the house. The high gloss and choice of colors recall Chinese art.

Originally taken over by New York City artists seeking more space and less rent, lofts have, since the sixties, become truly international. In this pure example in Antwerp, minimalist design results in a shed-like effect. Stripped down to the steel supports, the ceiling provides a distinctly low-tech touch. But the severe platform beds, the low walls beside the stairwell, and the industrial clothing racks are in keeping with the building's functional past.

(apartment continues overleaf)

Arrangement, illumination, and furnishing of the workroom *(overleaf, top left)* betray the influence of Le Corbusier. There is a play of textures: natural and neon light, carpeting, brick, and raw concrete.

This room is defined by the different shapes of the windows, the industrial ceiling supports, and the white brick walls *(overleaf, bottom left)*. The asymmetrical variations in light are equalized as simply as possible. The only movable objects are two Le Corbusier chrome-and-leather chairs.

A flight of concrete steps creates a sculptural focus in space *(overleaf, right)*. Beyond, two large white sofas form a convivial corner in the vastness of this former factory.

ngeniously backlit shelves provide a source of illumination in an otherwise dim—though dramatically shaped—upper story. The strong frame balances the massive half-timbering, while the horizontals and verticals lighten the plunging diagonals of the beams. Gerrit Rietveld's Red and Blue Chair, near the shelves, adds color; the rolled couch and chair-as-sculpture on the right soften the vast geometry of this space.

One could say that Dethleff Grüneke's house is all roof, above an apparently simple layout on either side of a central hall. The few pieces of furniture are white, black, or natural wood.

Sisal matting runs the entire length of the house. The double doors are of natural wood.

Grüneke designed his home to be a place of spacious diversity beneath its steeply sloping roof. Beams, rafters, and boards are all white; the built-in storage is minimally designed and functionally effective.

Spare, yet sensual, Grüneke's design for the guest bedroom relies upon rustic touches: the rough weave of the carpeting, a wicker basket, a cane chair. A small picture, placed next to the larger rectangle of the window, is a design element.

Like the couple who live here, these two workplaces celebrate unity and diversity. At first glance, this room seems to contain only an ormolu clock, a plant—and a one-legged black box. Not everything is built in, however: a second glance reveals the personal objects on the glass-topped desk.

Only a few feet away, the feeling of this space is entirely different. The massive, sculptural black desk faces away from the view; its curved base embraces a Classical statuette on the floor. Here, objects are grounded, instead of appearing to float in midair. Even the plants are different—no longer tropical, but desert succulents.

(apartment continues overleaf)

Here the designers meet. The summery orange Bertoia chairs cheerfully interrupt the pure whites, silvers, blacks, and transparents that continue out to the terrace—as does the owners' collection of art. The gentle view that sweeps to the hills delights the tired eye and refreshes the toiling spirit.

A large, sloping ceiling of polished wood and uncluttered floor space give this home a feeling of spaciousness. Above and beside the fourteen small windows a row of pictures creates a play of rectangles. It is a room of collections, with glass shelves contributing to a good-natured feeling in the space.

(overleaf)

Religious figurines and their accessories seem to float alongside a luminous stairwell. In silver frames, a collection of family photographs nestles under the deep, geometric cut of a window. The angle of the roof is borne by wedge shapes, in this white-on-white construction by architect and designer Peter Walser.

Marking the slope of the far wall of a cozy but luminous alcove is the emphasis on the window. Architect and designer Renato Severino's diagonal window seems to point to the energetic curve of the stairwell, which is echoed by the concave base of the wide modern sideboard. The neutral color scheme has been expanded to a natural one: dark brown and beige are joined by the pale green of the carpet and the malachite green of the sideboard.

Designed by M. Meiller, the home of Daniel and Claude Meiller is in Chalon-sur-Saône. The speckled wall treatment is carried over onto the bookshelves. The bedroom is doorless, its privacy derives instead from its situation at the end of the story, against an outside wall.

The bedroom is revealed as one area of a flow that incorporates the contemporary equivalent of a sitting room.

(apartment continues overleaf)

(continued from preceding spread)

A study and second bedroom adjoins the principal bedroom and is separated from the circulation area by a double-backed bookcase.

The rustic charms of the Burgundy countryside merge seamlessly with the Meillers' cosmopolitan flair and wit. The living room exhibits the wall treatment and exposed beams that unify the variously shaped areas throughout.

The attic is here reinterpreted in a very contemporary vein. Beneath a rolling sky, this found space is ready to be furnished with toys, shelves—and imagination!

B right and airy, this attic bathroom by
architect Klaus Bröckers rings elegant
changes on traditional white tile. The blond
wood places the design within a classic
Nordic context, with its blue sink and white
faucet as accents.

As early as the 1920s, the architect and designer Charles Édouard Jeanneret—better known as Le Corbusier—stated that a house should be a "machine for living." ❡ Today, when both time and space are precious, Le Corbusier's words sound prophetic. Efficiency, in everything from cars to toasters, is elegant, too. Industrial and decorative design merge. ❡ A room's purpose determines its design, and here imagination takes over. The most utilitarian spaces in the home are also proving to be the most inventive.

THE AESTHETICS OF FUNCTION

❡ In one kitchen, the service island is both absolutely practical and yet so rustic in appearance as to suggest the coziest of country kitchens. Or strip the island down to its most basic function, make it of wood, put drawers in it, utensils under it, and every food preparation task is easier. ❡ The lavish space of lofts can raise problems of heating and lighting—and inspire pleasing solutions. A two-way fireplace acts as a room divider, breaking space into more intimate units, heating two or more areas, and allowing light through. ❡ More and more we see multiple use expanding the functions of a space. Looking to institutional design, for example, we may isolate the fixtures in a bathroom into stalls. A dramatic black-and-white color scheme transforms its everyday white porcelain into striking graphic accents. ❡ A mirror can make the narrowest galley kitchen a pleasing place to work. In a living room, mirrors can both extend the apparent space and conceal built-in closets with little loss of actual space. ❡ Instead of concealing our possessions, we may want to store them out in the open. If we look to previously unexplored places, we may find areas high on walls, where a busy assemblage of antique evening purses becomes a delicate decorative array. A bookshelf and art space on a bedroom wall can turn into a headboard with evocative contours. ❡ A bedroom in levels can inconspicuously incorporate a desk. If we want to illuminate a single artlike piece of furniture in a shallow niche, why not set a vertical column of light alongside it? ❡ We need to study the use—or uses—to which a room will be put. But we must examine, too, our own personal and aesthetic requirements. When we know our needs, we can make virtues of them in practical and attractive rooms. ❡

(see picture on preceding spread)

Francesco Ridolfi, Patrizia Cagliani, and Luca de Padova, architects, designed a ''martyr's corner''—a workout area—in the bedroom of de Padova's Milan apartment. The outsize door is actually a panel that turns the room into a secret chamber. The handsome vertical stripes of the panel emphasize the graphic quality of the bars beside it— rather than their connotation of effort.

The bedroom *(above)* is reached through a mirrored panel in the architect's studio. Wood and other natural materials are mixed throughout the apartment with plastics, vinyls, and other manufactured materials. Similarly, angular shapes are mixed with curved contours, such as the bicycle tires, paper sunflower, and two-piece molded-plywood chaise longue.

I n New York City, a dining table that's like
a jigsaw puzzle counterpoints the colorful
play on dimensions juxtaposed on the wall.
Designer Michael de Santis has created an
environment that sets off the games.

Seemingly neutral, this area in designer Eva Jiricna's two-room London flat contributes to an overall impression of spaciousness. The rowing machine declares this a gymnasium, the folding table on the far wall makes it a dining room, the mirrored closets transform it into a dressing area. The far room is both studio and bedroom.

Mirrored closet doors amplify the apparent size of this area.

(apartment continues overleaf)

Jiricna imagined her living room as a combination swimming pool and conservatory. The resulting color palette was a successful alliance of an electric sapphire blue and bright green. The interior designer used the useful elements for texture: grids support wall lamps; vertical blinds transform the living room into a private guest room; narrow blinds control the degree of ambient light.

Easily maintained white porcelain tiles and the luxuriously comfortable deep tub are traditional elements in the bathroom. Designer Andrée Putman's decision to open the bathroom to the rest of Colette Bofill's loft—through the factory doors—allows sunlight to pour into the room and reflect pleasingly off the brilliant tile. The photographer's silver cloth on the couch beyond recalls the occupants' métier: advertising.

(apartment continues overleaf)

Only the ceiling betrays this room's industrial origins *(overleaf, top left)*. In the Bastille quarter of Paris, Putman has assembled a traditional conversation setting—fireplace and all. The Josef Hoffmann chairs and loveseat and the Eileen Gray rug bring personality to the corner of an expansive, airy space. A third Hoffmann chair extends the room into the meditation area.

This detail reveals the almost illusionistic use of space within space *(overleaf, bottom left)*. The elaboration and curves of the Hoffmann chairs provide an intriguing contrast to the powerful horizontal of the loft itself, and the harmonic verticals of the windows.

Comfort and minimalism merge in this airy, unbroken expanse *(overleaf, top right)*. The fireplace is the most essential of fireplaces; the living room contains a couch, a rug, and a table. But there is always room for the unexpected: the coffee table rests on toylike geometric solids, which in turn stand on a woolly black rug calibrated in white. The dining room chairs are the simplest, yet they allow guests to take their ease.

At first glance anonymously utilitarian, this kitchen *(overleaf, bottom right)* in fact fulfills two very traditional purposes: it is both a place to prepare meals and a place for friends to gather informally. The small-tiled floor is practical and also acts as a rug defining the space. The warm color of the counter, the visible shelving within, and the elegant curves of the chairbacks all conspire to render the kitchen invitingly domestic.

Milan's Piero Castellini arranges his rare books, pictures, and vases by horizontals and by clusters. The Max Ernst lithographs are attached by hinges to the shelves on the left, allowing access to the books behind them. The wall on the right, finished in a high gloss like the bookshelves, bears a chevron-shaped sculpture that varies the horizontals. It is, in fact, a coat rack designed by the decorator himself.

Three tiers of collections are stylish elements in the limited space of a New York City apartment. Architect Stephen Levine staged an elegant progression from the rich intricacy of turn-of-the-century silver mesh purses, to the lively variety of paperback books, to the sobriety of leatherbound volumes. Serenely spaced portraits, touches of mahogany, and knickknacks lend a Victorian hominess. The ladder on a track permits the collection to be varied at will.

Claudio Dini's own apartment in Milan is a successful example of functional simplicity that is also warm and inviting. The state of the original structure inspired Dini to install new floors, walls, ceilings—as well as all the built-ins—of chipboard. Finished with polyester paint in a mustard tone, this modest material acquired a luxurious, lacquered look that is also acoustically effective.

In the bedroom, an intriguing play of shelves, levels, and platforms incorporates a writing area for creative hours. The matting on the floor and the black accents carry throughout the apartment. A Vienna office chair is as much at home here as its fellows are in the dining room.

Walls and ceilings throughout this medieval Milanese tower, remodeled by architect Giuseppe Borgese, are ocher, the angles where they join, softened, as if with age. In the living room, the beam is updated in red. Red, too, is the spiral staircase leading to the roof terrace. Here, terra-cotta tiles bring in a traditional note.

(apartment continues overleaf)

Red accents throughout unify several rooms over three floors *(overleaf, left)*. In the bedroom, a red screen allows light into the dressing area. The window treatment recalls the building's history.

On the ground floor, the dining area shares a room with the kitchen *(overleaf, top right)*. The table is of pressed tin on a blond wood frame; the window treatment and red radiators reappear. Playful collections give this room its special charm.

The red note structures the kitchen *(overleaf, bottom right)*, where high-tech metal and blond wood join in amicable union. The counter serves as work surface and snack bar—and accommodates friends keeping the chef company.

Versatility in a service island is here charmingly illustrated in Ortwin Hillnhütter's version of the timeless country kitchen. At first glance, the natural wood and rough plaster suggest an almost quaint rusticity. Upon looking more closely, we discover an up-to-the-minute layout and choice of appliances. The open shelving combines ease of access with a cheerful busyness well suited to the room that is still the heart—if no longer the hearth—of the home.

This bedroom is all verticals and horizontals. Its apparent simplicity is, however, somewhat referential: the stepped outline of the bookcase recalls the height of Art Deco, the quartering of its sections, the architecture of casement windows. The negative space within the bookcase becomes a frame for a work of art hung inside.

A world in the finite space of a single room, this kitchen is all order, with few open shelves. The muted color scheme of blue gray, blue, and white rings unconventional changes on a traditional theme. The tile pattern, for example, has migrated to a tabletop. The task lighting focuses on work areas, keeping a warm atmosphere that ambient lighting might dilute.

The eating area, in the middle of the kitchen, is further accentuated by the large yellow light fixture suspended over it. The table is made of a beveled marble top mounted upon the frame of an old-style sewing machine. Outlined cabinets, door, and picture frames are a design motif. There is humor in the art hung low by the table: the picture on the left portrays a table and hanging lamp.

Like musical notes, black tiles are interspersed among white ones, just as the red dashes of the cabinet handles mitigate the otherwise all-white severity of this modern kitchen. Indeed, designer Peter Gergen has here successfully overlaid a contemporary galley kitchen onto traditional brick and timber. The effect, as exemplified in the range hood, is one of contrasting periods.

Yves Taralon integrated the solemnity of his "very Napoleon III" building with the expansiveness of pure space in this Japanese-inspired smoking room. The brass moldings are more emphatic versions of the strips that frame floor panels of rare Andean blue granite. The seating platform appears to float above a luminous bar.

Carl Hribar, a New York City architect, designed a shallow niche with a column of light beside it to accent the graceful chrome-and-black asymmetry of this classic Art Deco piece.

This bathroom bears little resemblance to conventional residential design. Its uncompromising functionality is heightened by the glare of bare neon. White tile on floor, ceiling, and walls speaks so shockingly of hygiene that the space becomes theatrical—a stage set of daily minimalist art.

Black and stark white transform conventional white fixtures into sculptural elements—and this bathroom into a space that is as dramatic as it is well planned. The shower is in the stall on the left, the toilet, in the one on the right. The soft carpet provides a sensuous contrast to the hard surfaces.

Function leads, and decoration follows, in this thoughtfully conceived galley kitchen. The double sink, the work space adjoining the range, and the built-in spice shelf are all planned for an active occupant. The tree-branch silhouettes are a gentle vision in a New York City apartment. The mirrored wall on the right widens the narrow space and enhances a combination work surface–breakfast counter with architect William Cohen's designer touch.

Architect and designer Alan Buchsbaum affixed a collapsible counter within the kitchen boundary described by the tile on the floor and the broad gray stripe on the ceiling. The counter's placement with respect to both kitchen and dining room multiplies its utility. It is a casual dinette for two, an additional work surface, as well as a sideboard for a more formal setting in the adjoining room. In the dining room, too, casters make the placement of the table more flexible.

In this New York City interior by architect William Cohen, a mirrored wall gives the room breadth and reflects natural light from the terrace. Although the built-ins appear strictly practical—and, indeed, bring order to a small space—open shelving displays a child's cherished possessions, thus declaring the room as unequivocally its occupant's.

Small as it is, this bathroom has space for art, both on the walls and in its brilliant details. The makeup table, with its collapsible mirror, slides out like a drawer from the sink counter. The stool that accompanies the makeup table is also collapsible. Every surface bears a luxurious gloss. The basin and faucets are as polished as the finest silver.

A century ago, a dwelling's layout depended upon the occupant's social class. Whether or not one had servants dictated how one's home worked. The kitchen, with its cooking smells and ongoing activity, was located well away from the dining room. ◫ Today, we are often the ones preparing meals for our family and friends, and we like to have company while we do it. So we build a dining room into a kitchen, with only a sliding panel to screen the mechanics. Conversely, we may fit a kitchenette into a sitting room–dining room area. ◫ In interior design, spatial composition is fundamental. With space at a premium, our architects and designers are reexamining conventional thinking—and finding it wanting. ◫ So, rather than sacrifice the original proportions of an old Italian country house by carving out a bathroom, the designer incorporated it into the bedroom, with a wooden cabinet as divider. In a small city space, only a low counter is the shared element between the bathroom and . . . the living room. (Sober, red-stained wood keeps surprise from turning into shock.) ◫ When space is ample, as in older apartment houses or lofts, we like to retain the flow of space. Reducing a supporting wall to a row of pilasters announces a distinction between rooms, while still allowing a grand sweep of distance. ◫ Platforms are useful devices for breaking a single large room into areas. An L-shaped, carpeted platform hosts an intimate conversation grouping, a plant corner, and even a futon seat that can double as a guest bed. ◫ The wide-open spaces of today's urban living are, of course, lofts. Often boasting fine wood floors, they tend to benefit from open-plan arrangements. When furniture groupings alone define the nature of the "room," the result can be very charming. ◫ Spaces flow not only horizontally but vertically. An open stairwell brings sunshine into a lower story, and provides a diagonal design element. A cantilevered, railless flight of steps reads graphically as a series of dashes leading to a secluded room beneath the rafters. ◫ Unifying factors can be as straightforward as carpeting, as dynamic as exposed half-timbering in an eighteenth-century carriage house, as subtle as matte black metal accents. ◫ *Something there is that doesn't love a wall. . . .* For some of us, Frost's line is profoundly true. Ultimately our homes are built of space, light, air—and of our notions of private and public rooms. ◫

SPACES IN SEQUENCE

(see picture on preceding spread)

A brightly skylit stairwell forms the core of a home designed by Möbel Behr. From the living room, the flow of space is horizontal—into the stairwell and past it to the kitchen—but also vertical, up the core to the second story.

In the built-in shelves *(top right)*, angles shape the rooms downstairs within a circular overall floor plan. Well worthy of its solitary splendor is the magnificent Baroque writing desk. In the foreground, the horizontals of couches and shelves convey soothing stability.

Oriental rugs on a carpet *(bottom right)* create a sensuous, ornate treatment that complements the horizontals and diagonals of the staircase's graphic profile.

Mario Tedeschi and Gianpaolo Monti devised a Milan living room that flows into the reading room on the right. The fireplace is understated, a black-framed oblong among others. Iron bands, like back-to-back Js on either side of the chimney stack, serve as shelves in niches.

(apartment continues overleaf)

The edges of arches and pillars are brilliantly beveled, the latter inset with matte black like the accents in the living room. In the reading room, these are replaced by Chinese-red lacquer, in keeping with the Oriental objects in the occupants' collections.

The bedroom's vaulted ceiling acts as a reprise of the arches in the other rooms. The carpet, too, carries through, its hue picked up in the glistening silk of the Balinese bedspread. Note also the matte black screen harking back to the living room.

With stylish wit, architect and interior designer Vittorio Gregotti closes an open bathroom with a ceiling-high door, its curved upper corner nestling into the juncture between wall and ceiling. From the living area, the handsome red-stained counter appears to be no more than that.

A single device—three bookshelves—transcends the diversity of functions to mark the length of the overall space. The wall treatment, more subdued, also declares this Milan apartment to be a single room.

The architect has taken full advantage of the old structure's thick walls: the pilaster alone sets the bedroom off—an architectural effect enhanced by the raised floor. In the simplicity of the room, the red-stained natural wood reappears. On the wall, the gilt elegance of an antique Persian door.

ae Aulenti took on a noble, turn-of-the-century apartment in Milan. This parlor is designed to accommodate a large number of family members and friends. Unconventionally, it is less formal than the living room. The gaze rises to the hunting scene that dominates the room; the round animal shapes are repeated in the soft curves of the comfortable furniture. A Victorian tradition lives on in the modestly covered tables.

(apartment continues overleaf)

Looking into the living room we see, at left and right, the detail of the speckled wall treatment *(overleaf, top left)*. The eye is carried to the magnificent fireplace, whose pattern becomes one of several in an otherwise severely unadorned space. In the tradition of the *palazzi*, "secret" doors are unobtrusively built into the walls.

Aulenti's idea was to allow a flow into an antiquated, boxy layout—despite supporting walls between the reception rooms *(overleaf, bottom left)*. The solution proved to be the "energetic presence," in Aulenti's words, of pilasters as deep as they are wide. The rooms are further unified by the blond-tobacco carpet—which sets off a fine collection of exotic rugs—and a color scheme that weds olive-green and brick-red accents.

Rosanna Monzini, a Milanese architect, created here an understated ambience. Guests on either side of the table enjoy the view of the greenery that surrounds the house. The room divider is finished with an antique speckling technique.

A shallow curve in the wall on the right defines the dining room, while the open monolith on the left not only acts as an additional sideboard, but also opens the eating area to the living room.

If the design of any New York City loft may be said to be "classical," architect Louis Meisel's home merits that description. The spacious horizontal plane of a sleeping platform shares a corner with shelves and stacks of Fiesta ware and other mass-produced American crockery of this century. Indeed, Americana is a fond motif throughout this SoHo space.

The palatial space around the table has definite boundaries: a column, the kitchen, bookshelves (behind which is the bedroom), and the track-lit wall of paintings. There is a balanced contrast, too, between the massive column and the beams of the spotlights.

(apartment continues overleaf)

The kitchen displays the low-key charm of once-upon-a-time America *(overleaf, top left)*. The lunch-counter effect is enhanced by the commercial, glass-doored refrigerator. Open shelves carry us back to the days of the general store.

Humor and hospitality characterize the dining area *(overleaf, bottom left)*. Nostalgia informs the art—especially the outsize gumball machines—that is visible from every point in the room. The director's chairs are in an "artificial" color; the table, in natural wood, harks back to the original factory floor.

An eat-in kitchen is not unusual; what is ingenious in this project by Bob Mayers, of the architectural firm of Mayers & Schiff, is a panel that slides out to screen the cooking island. The island incorporates not only the standard appliances, but a wine rack as well.

Two traditions are embodied here: that of the kitchen as common room, and the more modern one of kitchen as laboratory. The cylindrical base of the table adds formality, as does the curve of the table itself. When the panel is stowed, a difference in levels announces the difference in function.

Simply and brilliantly, two devices articulate this spacious kitchen by Mario Tedeschi and Gianpaolo Monti. The red line of tile is a strong horizontal element that unifies the room, while the freestanding unit situated on a gentle diagonal distinguishes the two areas.

The client, a Milanese lady, loves to prepare masterful creations for crowds of guests. This red-and-white breakfast area provides a cheerful environment for family meals and for planning sumptuous spreads.

Franco Menna's drafting studio occupies the ground floor of the designer's three-story home in Milan's Naviglio quarter, a few steps from Leonardo da Vinci's historic locks. The gray slate floor tiles are a unifying element throughout.

On the left is the office, and beyond it the bathroom. The ceiling treatment, in the diffuse illumination from wall-mounted uplights, adds sculptural interest to the right angles in the workrooms.

(apartment continues overleaf)

The second floor *(overleaf, left)*—with a glance down the broad stairwell—concludes in a roof-beamed corner that forms the living room. Soft pastels on the armchairs add touches of color, while an unconventional version of the traditional standing lamp abets the subtly domestic atmosphere.

Pastel pillows *(overleaf, top right)* recall the armchairs downstairs. The original post-horse stable from which Menna carved his home was two stories high. The designer gutted the building and created three stories: this charmingly intimate alcove nestles beneath the roof.

In the second-floor kitchen area *(overleaf, bottom right),* rectangles in two and three dimensions stand up to the otherwise dominant diagonal of the roof. The backsplash is of gray granite; the dark-gray steps are a floating graphic element that carries the floor treatment up to the sleeping loft.

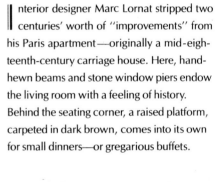

Interior designer Marc Lornat stripped two centuries' worth of "improvements" from his Paris apartment—originally a mid-eighteenth-century carriage house. Here, hand-hewn beams and stone window piers endow the living room with a feeling of history. Behind the seating corner, a raised platform, carpeted in dark brown, comes into its own for small dinners—or gregarious buffets.

Exposed half-timbering runs throughout the apartment. Lornat created a lightly structured space: translucent *shojis* screen the closet area on the left.

The raised floor emphasizes the already low ceilings. A wolfskin spread seems appropriate in the cavern-like space. Yet the open shelves and the flexibility of the sliding *shojis* keep any sense of confinement at bay.

From the platform beneath the windows, the play of levels is revealed. The oatmeal and dark-brown color scheme continues. Concealed behind the freestanding, chrome-framed shelving unit is the bedroom.

So deftly is actor Joel Grey's New York City living room divided into areas, that it easily accommodates a baby grand piano. Indeed, the piano itself becomes an area defined by the black wall hanging between two of the windows in this older building. Balancing it are two conversation groupings in neutral tones. The first focuses conventionally on the fireplace. The second occupies the shorter leg of the carpeted platform and creates an intimate room within a room. Wicker and plants enhance the airy brightness.

On the outskirts of Paris, a loft is home to designer Françoise Jourdan-Gassin and Bernard Lamarche-Vadel. This loft, however, eschews the industrial, in favor of Oriental carpets, wooden shelves and beams, and curtains theatrically parted before the flight of stairs leading to the bedroom and bathroom. The three painted flower pots are by Gasiorowski.

Inviting ease and friendly conversation in the couple's home is the pillowed comfort of a Le Corbusier sofa. On the left, the cut-out from the stairwell wall joins other right-angle shapes in a graphic array of geometric form.

(apartment continues overleaf)

(continued from preceding spread)

A skylight illuminates the kitchen and eating area and continues over the stairwell. The sparsely furnished rooms gain warmth from the Persian carpet and rust-red Pincemins painting. The dining table is an assembly of four schooldesks.

There is an often-neglected consideration that can make a great deal of difference in the final success (or otherwise) of our rooms: What do they say about us when we're not in them? What do they say about our preferences, our pleasures, our dreams, and our imaginations? ▨ No room that appears too carefully calculated can ever really take off. We may have a stunning white fireplace that sweeps its arcing hearth into the living room and sends its overmantel rising in columns like an organ. But place tiny chairs on the miniature steps of the overmantel, and suddenly they change the space around it, making it delightfully stamped with an imprint characteristic of the people who reside there. ▨ Why shouldn't kitchen shelves hang from rafters? It makes one stop and look, as well as leaving more free counter space besides. Perhaps we want to live in two places at once—New England and some mythical, ever-warm place. We can use a trompe l'oeil atrium in the dining room. A (real) rectangular rug points to the painted pool; a ficus tree and a green lacquer table emphasize the temperate-zone vegetation outside the window. ▨ Let us collect from the heart, let us listen to the voice of the child in us. When we add the dimension of informed judgment that we have acquired as adults, then we have taste in the fullest sense of the word. Two collectors of European avant-garde furniture of the last fifty years favor the whimsical. Kidney shapes of the fifties cohabit stylishly and humorously with the poker-faced Post-Modernism of Ettore Sottsass's Memphis design. ▨ Children are not only fanciful, they also feel things immediately and vividly, as artists often seek to. It can come as no surprise, then, to find an artist's apartment frankly rich with the primary colors and remembered emblems of childhood. ▨ Children also need freedom in their rooms, as well as structures that enable them to achieve the degree of order they (or their parents) like. A playroom with a modular ring of small chairs allows the tiny occupants great freedom of movement, while stating that the room is unequivocally *theirs*. ▨ As we assemble our rooms, let us be aware of all the resources available to us. Our rooms will reflect all we bring to them, and reward us with elegance, personality—and fun! ▨

FLIGHTS OF FANTASY

(see picture on preceding spread)

This area in an older building is dominated by the beams that separate the space into rooms. Beyond the structural partition, architect Dethleff Grüneke placed the dining room with its round table. The beams also serve as decorative and practical shelves.

A trompe l'oeil atrium *(top right)* startles and amuses in architect and designer Renato Severino's own home in Connecticut. More traditional elegance resides in the deep green of the lacquer table that collects the tints of the ficus beside it, and of the woods outside the window—the *real* window.

Deceptively spare, this room *(bottom right)* in Benjamin Baltimore's Paris apartment reveals its quirks and quandaries. A gray couch in an empty mauve space is the beginning. The mottled wall treatment calls attention to the stacked stone-sandwich coffee table, and to the blocky timepieces flanking the couch itself. Autumn leaves most often carpet a woodland floor. In all this urbanity, they rise to the ceiling.

William Cohen walks the frontiers of the absurd in search of fun, in this corner of an American home. He has taken nothing for granted: the bookcase is bowed, the vertical railings of the staircase are not just wrought—they are slightly overwrought. The rocking Mickey is in the same colors as Marilyn, asymmetrically placed and lit gallery-style. The comfy television room easily becomes a cozy guest alcove in this Western translation of a *tatami* room.

A stuffed panda keeps watch outside the French doors that lead from the living room into Keith Haring's New York City bedroom. The artist's own paintings hang on the walls. A tent makes a snug enclosure for a bed, within a shrewd clash of secondary colors. The television is co-opted as an element of active art.

The modestly domestic and gently retro Formica table and vinyl-backed chairs contrast with the screaming graffiti that cover even the refrigerator. Artist Haring loves life in the visual fast lane—his apartment is an orchestrated riot of color and image, a nonstop, constantly evolving neo-Dada festival.

(apartment continues overleaf)

(continued from preceding spread)

Haring's bright-yellow sitting room is a backdrop for a radiating hamburger, a Mickey
Mouse photo, and a lively assemblage of
other pictures. A portrait of the artist himself
is superimposed on Mobil Oil's flying horse.
Stimulus is everywhere: in the pulsing fluor-
escents of the sixties marshmallow chairs, in
the vibrating diagonals of the rug, in the hum
of the red, scalloped frame resting against
the wall.

Man Ray's atelier is a lively file of the late master's ideas. The pink sheets, flying like acrobats from the ceiling, both warm and diffuse the cold Paris light from the high industrial windows. Indeed, draped fabrics are a motif in this vast and comfortable room, befitting the theatrical genius of the godfather of Dada.

Jochem Jourdan and Bernhard Müller, architects with the Frankfurt firm PAS, designed an imaginative open-hearth fireplace for the home of Peter and Ulrike Berlipp. The mantel—or is it an overmantel?—creates a gently sophisticated focus for an informal living room. With equally Post-Modern whimsy, the family placed a collection of miniature chairs up the mantel's steps.

onsieur and Madame Yves and
Françoise Gastou traveled throughout
France and Italy assembling pieces from
every era, but especially from the fifties and
sixties. Here, in the hall and library of their
Paris home, a carpet by Alessandro Mandini
fetches us up to two of Matta's edition of six
jubilant chairs. By the window, the colors of a
Memphis/Sottsass bookshelf go well with
inset stained-glass crests.

(apartment continues overleaf)

A reading corner *(overleaf, top left)* in the
Gastou home is a Memphis/Sottsass set
piece of virtuoso antidesign. The chair is
a regal hallucination—the angles in the
bookshelf pick up the diagonals in the
parquet floor.

Striped in red and white, a glossy black table
(overleaf, bottom left) anchors the dining
room. Around it is a scattering of matte
black, molded polyurethane chairs. The cabinet, bearing some of the Gastous' collections,
is Sottsass's Factotum, since purchased by the
Museum of Fine Arts, Boston.

The Gastous inhabit their personal wonder-
land *(overleaf, right)* ''with subtle irony.''
They picked out the moldings around the dining room doorway in the brightest of lemon
yellows—a prologue to the gilt-framed mirror
above the mantel beyond. The yellow and
light-blue asymmetrical wing chairs are Paolo
Deganello's Torso. The cage is by André
Bloch, the carpet by Pati Mari. Instead of a
chandelier, Dali's *Soft Clock* of 1970 is suspended from a hanger.

177

M odern and traditional come together good-naturedly in this bright, well-planned family kitchen. The counter seats eight or more, and pure function ends in an abundance of glasses, spices, cups, tea canisters, and braids of garlic adorning the open hanging shelves.

B irds of paradise and primary colors, a
high ceiling—with fan—and stucco
walls lend this combination living room and
bedroom an insouciant, tropical flair. The
furniture is sparse: the couches, table, and
mirror are supplemented—if not overwhelmed—by massy green plants in huge
cachepots that themselves act as accessories.

If there were a Children's General Assembly, its headquarters might look something like this cheery, light-filled, top-story parlor. The wainscoting makes a cozy surround for the diminutive modular seating, adaptable to any configuration games might demand. Dolls mitigate the formality of wall-mounted brackets, and geometry reigns in feather-light Chinese lanterns and colorful pillars and posts.

Many of us like to be in touch with the great outdoors. No matter how passionately urban we may be, most of us have plants and seek systematically to make the most of the sunlight that finds its way between buildings to reach us. ▨ There are myriad ways our plants can be design elements, too. In an Italian home that looks out over a verdant courtyard, plants hanging from the high ceiling intensify the impression of greenery. ▨ Victorian conservatories have a sumptuous intimacy that we can bring

BRINGING THE OUTDOORS IN

into our homes. In an older building with a shallow ornamental balcony, a room is extended out to the wrought-iron railing, then glassed in. A row of colorfully leaved plants forms the lower frame, while slender trees, sporting their variety of foliage, edge the sides. Window seats for two and a games table complete this room within a room. ▨ The best feature of a compact city studio apartment is a window corner. The architect achieved two purposes with a single construction: a triangular "garden" between the windows. The platform is luxuriant with greenery that thrives in the abundant light, and at the same time it squares off the rest of the space, turning it into a conventionally proportioned living-and-sleeping room. ▨ Summer-house furniture endows any room with the ease of outdoor living. Wicker, stately bamboo, and a few judiciously placed plants can create the illusion of an English colonial verandah in a sunny London kitchen. ▨ What we won't do for light! One architect set a stepped series of windows into a wall, outlining the shape of a tree outside. The result is a wash of green-filtered sunshine. For some, the solution is to place skylights everywhere—even in the bathroom. ▨ For those who live in the suburbs or the country, whole walls of windows offer vistas of lawns and woods. For those rusticating in earnest, though, a wall of unplastered fieldstone provides texture in the main room of a small rural cottage—a look the owners enhance with a tabletop of weathered planks. ▨ In a contemporary Northern Italian country house, weathered and whitewashed struts evoke the simple life. But it is the brick flooring brought indoors that evokes summer even when the winter winds blow. ▨ Regardless of the climate we inhabit, or the setting—city or country—we reside in, we can integrate elements of our favorite seasons and places into the design of our home environments. ▨

(see picture on preceding spread)

Dramatic and dynamic, these intersecting I beams are surmounted by the repeating arches of a dried Japanese *sophora* tree. Architect Daniele Boatti was inspired by Italy's village pastures in the central carpeted square surrounded by gently rising steps and platforms. The ones on the right lead to the town on the hill—Boatti's sitting room and bedroom, lined with colorful works of art. At the same time, urbanity is present in the eighteenth-century Aubusson—which also provides the notes for the warm-toned color scale—and in Le Corbusier's chaise longue. The woodland theme reappears in the mushroom sculptures.

A miniconservatory *(above)* creates an intimate alcove with two plumply cushioned seats and a wrought-iron railing. GALLET, the design firm, extended the room and roofed the new area with glass. The foliage multiplies in the reflecting surface of the table, while the centerpiece continues the verdant theme.

Gae Aulenti designed an indoor garden
(above)—a triangular alcove in glass
and slate that modulates the monochrome
urban backdrop. Matchstick blinds transform
this one-room apartment from living room to
bedroom. Country accents abound—bamboo cachepots; a Sardinian carpet; a fringed,
hand-woven spread over a chaise longue as
wide as a double bed.

(overleaf)

The sweep of lawn and trees outside the
living room of this New England home
might easily have outweighed the interior
space, had New Haven architect and
designer Herbert Newman not carefully balanced its elements. Sturdy columns between
windows anchor the long curve of the exterior wall, while the massive leather couch on
the left acts as a counterweight to it. Similarly,
the narrow skylight above it sets off the room
and echoes the sky-filled outdoors. In such
spaciousness, the grand piano appears
almost delicate.

Highlights and skylights—on South Ocean Boulevard in Palm Beach. The living room of the Brimm house is lightly lush with subtropical colors and textures. Fresh yellows and greens and rattan furniture are in keeping with Florida's climate and culture.

Moldings on the cupboards of a sunny London kitchen are a formal backdrop for designer Franck Heroldt's delicate colonial touch. Plants in every corner draw attention to the luxuriance of the garden outside. A table of glass and wicker, and roomy bamboo chairs from a stately home echo distant memories of empire.

Graziella Lonardi's Rome apartment achieves an opulent feel with a few elements. Daylight glows down from a glass dome, as well as from the tall windows and door to the garden beyond. In the middle of the room stands a silver samovar. Around it, a collection of silver knickknacks gleams richly. The large room easily accommodates deep, outsize couches that emphasize its eight-sided shape. Andy Warhol's portrait of Lonardi balances the hues, from tobacco-brown rug to a ceiling full of hanging plants.

For years, designer Andrée Putman looked out of the windows of her eighteenth-century Paris apartment onto a small factory in the courtyard. When the property became available, Putman, the proprietor of Ecart International, purchased it—and transformed it. In the living room, Le Corbusier's chaise longue has pride of place. A skylight provides illumination.

Putman's Art Deco writing desk and its companion pieces are inlaid with ivory. The lemon cream of the walls reflects and warms the available light, while the open room arrangement and spare placement of furniture enhance the airy feeling and create a sculptural environment.

(apartment continues overleaf)

(continued from preceding spread)

Thonet chairs embrace a mirrored table from the thirties surmounted by a triptych by Françoise Jourdan-Gassin. The accessories are Bakelite and Baroque bronze objects. The rug is Eileen Gray's Blackboard.

A contemporary canopy of tinted mesh defines the sleeping space with the idea of privacy, but sunlight washes through the adjacent rooms.

Natural light pours in through a wall of glass doors, accentuating the few items that are not built in: the Bertoia bench in the foreground, the Le Corbusier loveseat in the background, and the antique armoire to the right. In this room by Peter Walser, one awakens with the day.

This indoor gazebo glows with natural light on even the gloomiest winter day. In his century-old villa in Lower Bavaria, architect Peter Lanz has devised a tranquil nook for dreaming—alone or à *deux*—reading, conversation, chess. The classical, trailing moldings are repeated in the ivy that frames the windows that in turn frame the spectacle of the changing seasons. The furniture is Josef Hoffmann.

U nplastered fieldstone masonry, a wood-
beamed ceiling, and a red-tiled floor
are the architectural elements that give this
bright living and dining room its country
flavor. Within the scheme, other design elements—the weathered planks of the table,
the brick placed as *objet* upon a shelf—cross
over to become decorative features.

etty Levine had carte blanche to design this house in Boca Raton, Florida, yet simplicity is the keynote. This glass-enclosed pool room feels like an outdoor terrace because of the weathered-teak furniture, whitewashed ceiling, and glazed-brick tiles.

The light-handed touch of the fine, woven-wood lattice is both surprising—like a grown-up's tree house—and attractive. Movable and economical, the screens invest an otherwise dead wall with eye-pleasing textures. On the right, they mask the kitchen. The Eero Saarinen table can accommodate a host of friends. The deeply coffered concrete ceiling keeps the room cool in the hottest summer days. Glazed black brick completes the rhythm of squares of different materials and dimensions.

Astute detail characterizes this arrangement. The marble, in warm tones, is artfully beveled, giving an impression of gleaming facets. There is a play of transparencies in the tinted shower screen, the vertical blinds that allow the glow of sunlight into the room, and the modish little chair. The more determined curves of the standing clothes hanger give it a sculptural quality.

Norbert Schütz employed materials more commonly used for exteriors in this cozy rural home. Stucco, pine, and bricks endow the semi-open plan with an illusive rusticity. In fact, the asymmetrical fireplace offers surfaces that support beloved pieces and plants, and the nook in front of the fire is set apart from the rest of the space by two steps, as well as by the short brick walls. The designer's art is, here, to *appear* artless.

This bathroom owes its attractiveness to several unconventional features. The uneven surface of the tiles gives the walls an importance not often found in this most utilitarian of spaces, an effect marked by quick accents in cream in the shower-and-bath. The most delightful notion was to install, directly over the shower, a skylight in the wood-paneled ceiling—which matches, nearly perfectly, the tiles on walls and floor.

Gae Aulenti exposed the structure of the ceiling, thus accentuating the height of this country home of a Milanese client. The brick floor and walls imbue the interior with a feeling of open air and a subtle touch of ancient Rome. The partition, divided by steps that lead to a reading platform, masks baths and bedrooms.

The spacious, year-round structure, located near Parma, combines handsome proportions and informal furnishings. The grid of windows front and back solved the problem of providing both illumination and privacy. The exposed beams are whitewashed, giving back light and suggesting the outdoors in their deceptively weather-beaten appearance. The kitchen is behind the freestanding wall at the back.

A rising series of tall rectangles describes, in hard-edged abstraction, the shape of the tree outside. Long draperies and low furniture further emphasize the ceiling's height. A reading lamp, also set low, the dark-stained parquet, and a vast paisley wall-hanging give the boxy space an intimate warmth.